Preston Prescott

All rights Reserved. No part of this publication or the information in it may be quoted from or reproduced in any form by means such as printing, scanning, photocopying or otherwise without prior written permission of the copyright holder.

Disclaimer and Terms of Use: Effort has been made to ensure that the information in this book is accurate and complete, however, the author and the publisher do not warrant the accuracy of the information, text and graphics contained within the book due to the rapidly changing nature of science, research, known and unknown facts and internet. The Author and the publisher do not hold any responsibility for errors, omissions or contrary interpretation of the subject matter herein. This book is presented solely for motivational and informational purposes only

Contents

Other Books by the Author 1

Chapter 1: Introduction to SQL & Databases 2

Chapter 2: Data Types & Database/Table Creation 9

    Exercise 2 17

Chapter 3: Drop, Alter, Truncate, & Insert 19

    Exercise 3 25

Chapter 4: Select, Where, & Order By 27

    Exercise 4 34

Chapter 5: SQL Operators I 35

    Exercise 5 42

Chapter 6: SQL Operators II 43

    Exercise 6 51

Chapter 7: Aggregate Functions, Delete, & Update 53

    Exercise 7 62

Chapter 8: Relationships & Join Queries 64

    Exercise 8 80

Chapter 9: SQL Sub-queries 82

    Exercise 9 85

Chapter 10: SQL Character Functions 86

    Exercise 10 89

Other Books by the Author 91

Other Books by the Author

JavaScript Programming: A Beginners Guide to the Javascript Programming Language
http://www.linuxtrainingacademy.com/js-programming

If you've attempted to learn how to program in the past, but hadn't had much success then give *JavaScript Programming* a try. It will teach you exactly what you need to know about programming in the world's most widely used scripting language in existence today. It will start you at the beginning and allow you to build upon what you've learned along the way.

Chapter 1: Introduction to SQL & Databases

SQL stands for structured query language. It is officially pronounced as "Ess que ell." SQL, as the name suggests, is a query language used to interact with relational databases. SQL is used to perform functions like inserting data into a database, retrieving data, updating data, deleting data, and other similar actions. The first chapter presents a bird's-eye view of SQL along with a brief introduction to databases.

Contents

- What are databases?
- Advantages of relational databases
- Types of SQL
    I. Data Definition Language
    II. Data Manipulation Language

1- What are Databases?

A software application needs to store data. There are two ways to store the data used by any application. Your first option is to store it in the application's memory where data resides as long as the application is running. The other option is to store data on your hard disk and then, via some procedure, fetch the data into the memory of the computer and perform a transaction on the data. The random access memory of a computer is limited; if the data that has to be processed by the application is huge, all of it cannot be simultaneously stored in memory. In such scenarios, a second storage option is required.

On a hard disk, data can be stored in different file formats. It can be stored in the form of text files, word files, mp4 files, etc. However, a uniform interface that can provide access to different types of data under one umbrella in a robust and efficient manner is required. Here, the role of databases emerge.

Definition: "A collection of information stored in computer in a way that it can easily be accessed, managed and manipulated."

Databases store data in the form of a collection of tables where each table stores data about a particular entity. For instance, if you are developing an application which stores records of students of a university, it will have a table that contains records of students and a table which contains records of courses. The information that we want to store about students will be represented in the columns of the table. Each row of the table will contain the record of a particular student. Each record will be distinguished by a particular column, which will contain a unique value for each row.

Suppose you want to store the ID, name, age, gender, and department of a student. The table in the database that will contain data for this student will look like the one below:

SID	SName	SAge	SGender	SDepartment
1	Tom	14	Male	Computer
2	Mike	12	Male	Electrical
3	Sandy	13	Female	Electrical
4	Jack	10	Male	Computer
5	Sara	11	Female	Computer

Student Table

Here, the letter "S" has been prefixed with the name of each column. This is just one of the conventions used to denote column names. You can give any name to the columns. (We shall see how to create tables and columns within it in the coming chapters.) It is much easier to access, manipulate, and manage data stored in this form. SQL queries can be executed on the data stored in the form of tables having relationships with other tables.

A database doesn't contain a single table. Rather, it contains multiple tables with relationships between them. Relationships maintain database integrity and prevent data redundancy. For instance, if the school decides to rename the Computer department from "Computer" to "Comp & Soft," you will have to update the records of all students in the Computer department.

You will have to update the 1st, 4th, and 5th records of the student table.

It is easy to update three records; however, in real life scenarios, there are thousands of students and it is an uphill task to update the records of all these students. In such scenarios, relationships between data tables become important. For instance, to solve the aforementioned redundancy problem, we can create another table named Department and store the records of all the departments in that table. This table will look like this:

DID	DName	DCapacity
101	Electrical	800
102	Computer	500
103	Mechanical	500

Department Table

Now, in the student table, instead of storing the department name, the department id will be stored. The student table will be updated as follows:

SID	SName	SAge	SGender	DID
1	Tom	14	Male	102
2	Mike	12	Male	101

3	Sandy	13	Female	101
4	Jack	10	Male	102
5	Sara	11	Female	102

Table Student

It can be seen that the department name column has been replaced by the department id column, represented by "DID". The 1st, 4th, and 5th rows that previously were assigned the department "Computer" now contain the id of the department, which is 102. Now, if the name of the department is changed from "Computer" to "Comp & Soft", this change has to be made only in one record of the department table and all the associated students will be automatically referred to the updated department name.

2- Advantages of Databases

The following are some of the major advantages of databases:

- Databases maintain data integrity. This means that data changes are carried out at a single place and all the entities accessing the data get the latest version of the data.
- Through complex queries, databases can be efficiently accessed, modified, and manipulated. SQL is designed for this purpose.
- Databases avoid data redundancy. Through tables and relationships, databases avoid data redundancy and data belonging to particular entities resides at single place in database.

- Databases offer better and more controlled security. For example, usernames and passwords can be stored in tables with excessive security levels.

3- Types of SQL Queries

On the basis of functionality, SQL queries can be broadly classified into a couple of major categories as follows:

- **Data Definition Language (DDL)**

Data Definition Language (DDL) queries are used to create and define schemas of databases. The following are some of the queries that fall in this category:

I. CREATE – to create tables and other objects in database
II. ALTER – to alter database structures, mainly tables.
III. DROP - delete objects, mainly tables from the database
IV. TRUNCATE - removes all records from a table, including all spaces allocated for the records
V. COMMENT - add comments to the data dictionary
VI. RENAME – rename tables or other objects.

- **Data Manipulation Language**

Data Manipulation Language (DML) queries are used to manipulate data within databases. The following are some examples of DML queries.

I. SELECT – select data from tables of a database
II. INSERT - insert data into a database table
III. UPDATE - updates the existing data within a table
IV. DELETE - deletes all rows from a table, the space for the records remains.

Chapter 2: Data Types & Database/Table Creation

This chapter presents a brief introduction to different data types. "Data types" refers to formats in which data is stored in a database. For instance, if you want to store the name of a person, it will be stored in "varchar" format in the database. Similarly, the id or age of a person is stored in integer format. Data types vary depending on the type of database server. However, basic data types are uniform in different servers. Later in this chapter, I will show you how you can create databases and database tables via SQL queries.

Contents

- **SQL Data types**
- **Creating a Database**
- **Creating Tables in a Database**

1- SQL Data Types

- **Exact Numeric Data Types:**

The following are the SQL data types that store exact numeric data:

DATA TYPE	FROM	TO
bigint	-9,223,372,036,854,775,808	9,223,372,036,854,775,807
int	-2,147,483,648	2,147,483,647
smallint	-32,768	32,767
tinyint	0	255
bit	0	1
decimal	-10^38 +1	10^38 -1
numeric	-10^38 +1	10^38 -1
money	-922,337,203,685,477.5808	+922,337,203,685,477.5807
smallmoney	-214,748.3648	+214,748.3647

- **Approximate Numeric Data Types:**

The following are the SQL data types that store approximate numeric data:

DATA TYPE	FROM	TO
float	-1.79E + 308	1.79E + 308
real	-3.40E + 38	3.40E + 38

- **Sql Date and Time Data Types**

These are some of the SQL date and time data types:

DATA TYPE	FROM	TO
Datetime	Jan 1, 1753	Dec 31, 9999
Smalldatetime	Jan 1, 1900	Jun 6, 2079
date	Stores a date like October 10, 1991	
time	Stores a time of day like 11:30 P.M.	

- **String Data Types**

The following are SQL String data types:

DATA TYPE	FROM	TO
char	char	Maximum length of 8,000 characters. (Fixed length non-Unicode characters.)
varchar	varchar	Maximum of 8,000 characters. (Variable-length non-Unicode data.)
varchar(max)	varchar(max)	Maximum length of 231 characters, Variable-length non-Unicode data (SQL Server 2005 only).
text	text	Variable-length non-Unicode data with a maximum length of 2,147,483,647 characters.

2- Creating a Database

Though most database servers come with tools that allow users to create databases via the GUI interface, the backend query which actually creates the database at the server is the same. To create a new database, simply open the query window of the database server you are using. For demonstration, I am using MS SQL Server Express 2014.

Note: All the queries executed in this book follow Transact SQL (T-SQL) standards. Also note that SQL statements are case insensitive; therefore, I will execute some queries in capital case and some in lower case just to demonstrate its case insensitivity.

Enter the following query in your query window:

Query 1:

```
CREATE DATABASE Hospital;
```

This query will create a database named "Hospital" on the instance of the database server you are using. Now, if you want to see if your database has been created, you can type the following command in your query window.

Query 2:

```
SELECT name
FROM sys.databases
```

When Query 2 is executed, the output window will display a list of all the existing databases on your database server. This is the output of the query:

name
master

tempdb
model
msdb
MyDB
SchoolDB
Hospital

You can see "Hospital" in the last row. Your output might be different depending upon the number of databases you have already created. Let's have a look at what's happening in the the second query.

Here, I am using a "SELECT" statement to select the name of the databases "FROM" the database which resides on this system. In the SQL server, the database instance itself is considered a top level database which contains several user defined databases. Here, "sys.databases" refers to a list of all the databases residing on this system. We shall see the uses of "SELECT" and "FROM" statements in detail in later sections.

Let's now try to get the database id and the creation date of all the databases.

Query 3

```
SELECT name, database_id, create_date
FROM sys.databases
```

See here, in addition to name we are also selecting database_id and create_date. In the output, you shall see all of these properties. The output is as follows. You can see the date of creation of your database along with the database id, which is internally assigned to every database that's created on a DB server. (Database is often referred to as DB.)

name	database_id	create_date
master	1	2003-04-08 09:13:36.390
tempdb	2	2015-02-01 09:08:30.663
model	3	2003-04-08 09:13:36.390
msdb	4	2014-02-20 20:49:38.857
MyDB	5	2015-01-27 01:20:59.790
SchoolDB	6	2015-01-29 00:27:27.153
Hospital	7	2015-02-01 12:39:42.703

3- Creating Tables in a Database

Once you have set up your database, the next step is to create tables in the database because, ultimately, you will have to store your data in tables. To create tables in any database server, you have to perform a couple of steps. First, you will need to switch to the database in which you want to create your table. We saw in the last section that a server can host multiple databases; therefore, it is important to specify the database where you want to create your table. The following query switches query editor to execute queries on the "Hospital" database, which we created in the last section.

Query 4

```
USE Hospital
GO
```

Now, all queries executed in the query window will operate on the "Hospital" table. Suppose we want to create a table named "Patient" in the "Hospital" database. Patient has an id, name, age, and disease description attribute. The following query creates a table which stores this data.

Query 5

```
CREATE TABLE Patient
    (PatientID int PRIMARY KEY NOT NULL,
    PatientName varchar(50) NOT NULL,
    PatientAge int NULL,
    DiseaseDescription text NULL)
```

The query might look intimidating at first, however it's pretty simple. "CREATE TABLE" is the statement which is used to create any table in the database, followed by the table name. Inside the round opening and closing brackets, you specify the columns of the table and their characteristics. The statement "PatientID int PRIMARY KEY NOT NULL" states that a column named "PatientID" will be created and this column should store integer type data. The flag "PRIMARY KEY" refers to the fact that this column holds a primary key and value, for this column cannot be null. In the same way, "PatientName", "PatientAge", and "DiseaseDescription" columns have been added. Here, the concept of the primary key needs to be elaborated.

- **Primary Key**

The primary key is basically a column which uniquely distinguishes a record or row in a database. No two records in a table can have the same primary key. Also, the primary key can never be null.

In Query 5, we have specified PatientID as the primary key, which means no two patients can have same primary key.

Now, to see if the "Patient" table has been created in the "Hospital" database, simply execute the following query:

Query 6

```
SELECT name
FROM sys.tables
```

You must set "Hospital" as the current database executing the above query. See Query 4 for switching databases.

Exercise 2

Task:

Create a database named "Organization" and, inside the database, create a table named Employee. Employee should have an Id (which should be the primary key), Name, Age, and Salary. Salary and Age can contain null values.

Solution

Creating the Organization Database

```
CREATE DATABASE Organization;
```

Switching to the Organization DB

```
USE Organization
GO
```

Creating the Employee Table

```
CREATE TABLE Employee
    (EmployeeID int PRIMARY KEY NOT NULL,
    EmployeeName varchar(50) NOT NULL,
    EmployeeAge int NULL,
    EmployeeSalary money NULL)
```

Chapter 3: Drop, Alter, Truncate, & Insert

In chapter 2, we studied how to create a database and how to create tables within that database. We also looked at some of the basic data types in SQL. In this chapter, we are going to study Drop, Truncate, Alter, and Insert statements. A drop statement is used to delete a Table or Database. Alter is primarily used to modify the structure of a table. Truncate is used to delete all the data from the table. We shall also study the insert query, which is used to insert data into the table.

Contents

- **Drop Statement**
- **Truncate Statement**
- **Alter Statement**
- **Insert Statement**

1- **Drop Statement**

A drop statement is used to drop or delete a database or table and all of its associated data, constraints, indexes, and triggers. Before executing a Drop Table query, first create another table inside the "Hospital" database, which we created in the last chapter. Name the table "Department". It should have columns for id, name, and capacity. The following query would create this table.

```
CREATE TABLE Department
    (DepartmentID int PRIMARY KEY NOT NULL,
    DepartmentName varchar(50) NOT NULL,
    DepartmentCapacity int NULL)
```

Now, if you view the tables in the "Hospital" DB, it should contain two tables named "Patient" and "Department". Suppose we want to delete the "Patient" table from the DB; we can use Drop Table statement. The following Drop Table query deletes the "Patient" table from the Hospital DB.

Query 1:

```
DROP TABLE Patient
```

Remember, SQL queries are case insensitive; to delete the table, you can use both lowercase "drop table" and uppercase "DROP TABLE" followed by the table name. Now, if you list all the tables in the "Hospital" DB, you will not see the "Patient" table. To delete the whole Hospital database, you can simply use the following statement.

Query 2:

```
Drop Database Hospital
```

2- Truncate Statement

The truncate statement deletes all the data inside the table without deleting the table itself. In fact, the truncate statement deletes the table, including the data inside it, and then recreates an empty table. To truncate the "Patient" table, you can use following statement:

Query 3:

```
TRUNCATE TABLE Patient
```

3- Alter Statement

The alter statement is used to modify the structure of a table in the database. Using an alter statement, you can add, remove, or update an existing column of a table.

- **Adding a Column in a Table**

Suppose you want to add the patient's date of birth in the "Patient" table we created in the last chapter. You can use an alter statement as follows:

Query 4:

```
ALTER TABLE Patient
```

```
ADD PatientDOB date
```

The syntax of an alter statement is simple. You have to write "ALTER TABLE" followed by the table name. Next, you have to write ADD followed by the name of the column you want to add and its data type. In Query 4, we added the PatientDOB column of type date.

You can view all the columns inside the "Patient" table using following query:

Query 5

```
SELECT COLUMN_NAME
FROM Hospital.INFORMATION_SCHEMA.COLUMNS
WHERE TABLE_NAME = N'Patient';
```

You will see the following output:

COLUMN_NAME
PatientID
PatientName
PatientAge
DiseaseDescription
PatientDOB

You can see the newly added DOB column in the last row.

- **Deleting a Column from a Table**

The alter statement can be used to delete a particular column from a table. For instance, if you want to delete "DiseaseDescription" column from the "Patient" table, you can use following query:

Query 6:

```
ALTER TABLE Patient
DROP COLUMN DiseaseDescription
```

The first part of the query is similar to that of adding a column. However, in the second part, we use "DROP COLUMN" followed by the name of the column which we want to delete.

- **Modifying a Table column**

Finally, an alter statement can also be used for modifying a particular table column. We specified the data type of PatientName as varchar(50). If we want to change it to varchar(100) and allow it to contain null values, we can use an alter statement. The following query demonstrates this:

Query 7:

```
ALTER TABLE Patient
ALTER COLUMN PatientName varchar(100) NULL
```

4- Insert Statement

We have learned to create a database, we know how to create and delete tables, and we know how to modify table structure. Now it's time to insert some dummy data in the tables we created. Before executing insert queries, make sure you have created the "Hospital" database (refer to chapter 1) which contains the "Patient" table. The columns of the "Patient" table are as follows:

COLUMN_NAME
PatientID
PatientName
PatientAge
DiseaseDescription

To insert data into the "Patient" table, have a look at Query 8.

Query 8:

```
INSERT INTO Patient VALUES (100, 'James', 10, 'Heart Disease')
```

To insert data in any table, we have to use "INSERT INTO" followed by the table name and then "VALUES" followed by the value to be inserted, separated by a comma inside the closing bracket. It is important to remember that the order in which values are inserted should match the order of the columns in the table. For instance, the first column in the "Patient" table is PatientID, which stores integer type data; therefore, we inserted an integer, 100, as the first value to be inserted. The second column is PatientName; therefore we inserted a string "James" and so on.

- **Changing the order of inserted values**

You can also change the order in which you want to insert the values in a table. For that purpose, you have to mention the order in opening and closing round brackets after the table name. For example, take a look at the following query:

```
INSERT INTO Patient(PatientName, PatientID,
DiseaseDescription, PatientAge)
    VALUES ('Mike', 101, 'Lung Disease', 25)
```

You can see that in the specified order, PatientName comes first, followed by PatientID, DiseaseDescription, and PatientAge. Therefore, the values are inserted according to this modified order, where Mike comes first, followed by 101 and so on.

Exercise 3

Task:

Alter the "Patient" table by removing the PatientAge column and add a Patient's Blood group column. Insert some data in the modified table.

Solution

Removing the PatientAge Column

```
Alter table Patient
Drop Column PatientAge
```

Adding the Patient Blood Group Column

```
Alter table Patient
Add PatientBG varchar(10)
```

Inserting Data into the Modified Table

```
INSERT INTO Patient VALUES (100, 'James', 'Heart Disease','B+')
```

Chapter 4: Select, Where, & Order By

We have learned how to create databases, how to create a table in a database, and how to alter its structure. We also know how to insert data into tables. However, we still don't know how to read from the table. In most software applications, data reading and its representation is a pivotal task. Fortunately enough, SQL comes with queries and operators which, when used together, help us retrieve the desired set of data from the database. In SQL, the "SELECT" statement is used to retrieve data from database, the "Where" clause is used for conditional retrieval of data, and the "Order By" clause is used to change the order in which data records are fetched. In this chapter, we shall see these concepts in action.

Contents

- **SELECT Statement**
- **Where Clauses**

- Order By

1- SELECT Statement

Before executing a SELECT statement on the database, let us insert a few records in the "Patient" table, which we created in the last chapter. Your "Patient" table should have four columns: PatientID, PatientName, PatientAge, DiseaseDescription. Execute the following query to insert five records into the "Patient" table.

Query 1

```
INSERT INTO Patient VALUES
(101, 'James', 10, 'Heart Disease'),
(150, 'Sarah', 15, 'Lung Disease'),
(245, 'Isaac', 21, 'Kidney Disease'),
(250, 'Mike', 17, 'Ear Infection'),
(301, 'Maria', 6, 'Nose Injury')
```

This above query will insert five records in the "Patient" table. This is the way to insert multiples in tables through use of a single query.

If we want to select all of these records, we can execute the following SELECT statement:

Query 2

```
SELECT * FROM Patient
```

The syntax of the SELECT query is the simplest of all the queries we have executed up till now. To select all the records from a table, the use the "SELECT * FROM" query followed by the table name from which you want to retrieve records. For instance, I wanted to retrieve all the records from the "Patient" table, so I executed Query 2. The output of Query 2 would be a set of rows containing all the records in the "Patient" table, as shown below:

PatientID	PatientName	PatientAge	DiseaseDescription
101	James	10	Heart Disease
150	Sarah	15	Lung Disease
245	Isaac	21	Kidney Disease
250	Mike	17	Ear Infection
301	Maria	6	Nose Injury

You can see that all the records we inserted in the "Patient" table using Query 1 have been retrieved using the SELECT statement in Query 2.

The asterisk which follows the SELECT keyword retrieves all the columns in the table. What if you want to retrieve only PatientName and PatientAge of all the patients in the "Patient" table? Don't worry, it's pretty simple; you will have to modify the SELECT statement as follows:

Query 3

```
SELECT PatientName, PatientAge FROM Patient
```

In Query 3, the asterisk has been replaced by the column names of the table. The above query will retrieve values from the PatientName and PatientAge column of all the records in the "Patient" table. The output of Query 3 is as follows:

PatientName	PatientAge
James	10
Sarah	15
Isaac	21
Mike	17
Maria	6

- **Using As with Select Statement**

If you see the output of Query 2 and Query 3, you will see that the table headers are not appropriate. It is okay to have a column in the database named PatientName with no spaces between Patient and Name. However, this doesn't look appropriate in the output. You can change the column names in the output using the "AS" keyword in select statement. For instance, if you want to change the name of the PatientName column to "Patient Name" and PatientAge column to "Patient Age" in the output, you need to modify the SELECT statement as follows:

Query 4

```
SELECT PatientName AS 'Patient Name', PatientAge AS
'Patient Age' FROM Patient
```

The output of Query 4 will be the following set of records:

Patient Name	Patient Age
James	10
Sarah	15
Isaac	21
Mike	17
Maria	6

2- **Where Clauses**

In real time applications, you don't often want to retrieve all the records in the database. You only want records that satisfy some criteria. For instance, you may want to get the records of patients over the age of 10. This is where "Where" clauses come into play. Have a look at Query 5 to see where clause in action.

Query 5

```
SELECT * FROM Patient
```

```
WHERE PatientAge>10
```

The syntax of a "where" clause is straight forward. You have to use the word "Where" followed by the condition that you want your data to satisfy. We wanted to retrieve records where PatientAge was greater than 10, therefore we used the condition "PatientAge > 10". Here, the symbol ">" is the SQL operator. We will see different SQL operators in detail in the next chapter. The output of Query 5 will be a set of all records in the "Patient" table where the patient's age is greater than 10. This is as follows:

PatientID	PatientName	PatientAge	DiseaseDescription
150	Sarah	15	Lung Disease
245	Isaac	21	Kidney Disease
250	Mike	17	Ear Infection

3- Order By

The "order by" clause is used to change the order in which records are retrieved from the database. If you want to retrieve the records of all patients from the "Patient" table in alphabetical order of names, you can use the "order by" clause. The following query demonstrates the usage of "order by" clauses:

Query 6

```
SELECT * FROM Patient
Order by PatientName
```

The output would be a record of all the patients in the "Patient" table arranged in alphabetical order.

PatientID	PatientName	PatientAge	DiseaseDescription
245	Isaac	21	Kidney Disease
101	James	10	Heart Disease
301	Maria	6	Nose Injury
250	Mike	17	Ear Infection
150	Sarah	15	Lung Disease

You can fetch the records of patients in reverse alphabetical order by appending "Desc" after the "order by" clause. This will fetch records in descending alphabetical order. The following query demonstrates this:

Query 7

```
SELECT * FROM Patient
Order by PatientName Desc
```

The output of Query 7 would be as follows:

PatientID	PatientName	PatientAge	DiseaseDescription
150	Sarah	15	Lung Disease
250	Mike	17	Ear Infection
301	Maria	6	Nose Injury
101	James	10	Heart Disease
245	Isaac	21	Kidney Disease

Exercise 4

Task:

From the "Patient" table, select PatientName and DiseaseDescription of patients with ages less than 20 years. Order the results in descending order of Age.

Solution

```
SELECT PatientName, DiseaseDescription from Patient WHERE PatientAge < 20 Order by PatientAge Desc
```

Chapter 5: SQL Operators I

In chapter 4, we studied the usage of "where" clauses. We saw how we can retrieve the desired records based on a particular condition using a "where" clause. SQL operators are basically keywords or characters that are used to specify a condition in a "where" clause. For instance, in chapter 4, we used a greater than ">"operator to fetch all the patient records where the age was greater than 10. In chapters 5 and 6, we shall see some of the most commonly used SQL operators.

SQL operators can be broadly categorized into four groups:

- Comparison Operators
- Logical Operators
- Conjunctive Operators
- Negation Operators
- Arithmetic Operators

In this chapter, we shall see the workings of Comparison and Logical Operators. In the next chapter, we shall study the remaining three operator types.

1- Comparison Operators

There are six types of SQL comparison operators:

I. Equality (=)
II. Non-equality (<>)
III. Less Than Values (<)
IV. Greater Than Values (>)
V. Less than equal to (<=)
VI. Greater than equal to(>=)

We shall demonstrate the usage of Non-Equality operators in Query 1 of this chapter. Suppose you want to fetch the records of all patients except those who are age 17; you can try non-equality operator as follows:

Query 1

```
SELECT * from Patient
where PatientAge <> 17
```

This query will retrieve records of all the patients except the patients with ages equal to 17. I advise you to try the remaining comparison operators yourself. They are pretty straight forward and self-explanatory.

2- Logical Operators

Following are the SQL logical operators:

I. IS NULL

II. BETWEEN
III. IN
IV. LIKE
V. DISTINCT
VI. EXISTS
VII. ALL and ANY

In this chapter, we will cover the first five operators.

- **IS NULL**

The IS NULL operator is used to fetch all records from the table where a particular column has a null value. For instance, if you want to retrieve all the records from the "Patient" table where DiseaseDescription has a null value, you can use the following query:

Query 2

```
SELECT * from Patient
where DiseaseDescription is null
```

You will not see any records in the output since all of the patient records that we inserted in the "Patient" table contained some value for the DiseaseDescription column.

- **BETWEEN**

The BETWEEN operator is used to filter records having particular column values between a specified range. For instance, if you want to retrieve the records of patients with ages greater than or equal to 10 and less than or equal to 20, you can use the BETWEEN operator as follows:

Query 3

```
SELECT * from Patient
where PatientAge between 10 and 20
```

The output records are as follows:

PatientID	PatientName	PatientAge	DiseaseDescription
101	James	10	Heart Disease
150	Sarah	15	Lung Disease
245	Isaac	21	Kidney Disease
250	Mike	17	Ear Infection

- **IN**

The IN operator is used to compare a particular column value with a list of values. The records whose column values match one of the values in the list are returned. For instance, if you want to retrieve the records of patients where the PatientID is equal to 101, 245, or 301, you can use the IN operator as follows:

Query 4

```
SELECT * from Patient
where PatientID IN(101,245,301)
```

In the output, you will see the patient records with PatientIDs equal to 101, 245, or 301.

PatientID	PatientName	PatientAge	DiseaseDescription
101	James	10	Heart Disease
245	Isaac	21	Kidney Disease
301	Maria	6	Nose Injury

- **LIKE**

The LIKE operator is used to compare values in a particular table column with similar values using some wild card operators. There are two wild card operators used with LIKE operators: percentage (%) and underscore (_).

The LIKE operator is one of the most widely used SQL operators. For instance, if you are implementing a search functionality in your application where you retrieve records based on a similar string entered in a text box and the database values, one of the solutions is to use LIKE operators. Let's see a simple example where PatientName contains a string "sa".

Query 5

```
SELECT * from Patient
where PatientName LIKE('%sa%')
```

This query will retrieve the records of all the patients where the PatientName contained a string "sa". Two patients, Sarah and Isaac, fulfill this criterion. The output would be as follows:

PatientID	PatientName	PatientAge	DiseaseDescription
150	Sarah	15	Lung Disease
245	Isaac	21	Kidney Disease

In the last query, we specified "sa" between two percentage signs. This means that the "sa" string can occur anywhere within the PatientName value. If you want to retrieve records of all the patients where the PatientName starts with "sa" you can use a LIKE operator as follows:

Query 6

```
SELECT * from Patient
where PatientName LIKE('sa%')
```

Since, Sarah is the only patient whose name starts with "sa", hers is the only record which will be retrieved.

The underscore operator represents a single character. For instance, if you want to retrieve the records of all patients with an "a" in the second position in their name, you can use a combination of "_" and "%" operators as follows:

Query 7

```
SELECT * from Patient
where PatientName LIKE('_a%')
```

The above query implicates that, no matter what character is at the first position in the name, records of patients with the character "a" in the second position will be returned. The output of the above query is as follows:

PatientID	PatientName	PatientAge	DiseaseDescription
101	James	10	Heart Disease
150	Sarah	15	Lung Disease
301	Maria	6	Nose Injury

- **DISTINCT**

The DISTINCT operator is used to retrieve DISTINCT values of a particular column from a database. For instance, if you want to retrieve all the unique values of the PatientName column from the database, you can use the DISTINCT operator as follows:

Query 8

```
SELECT DISTINCT PatientName from Patient
```

Exercise 5

Task:

From the "Patient" table, select the records of all the patients where PatientName ends with "sa" and has "n" in the third position:

Solution

```
SELECT * FROM Patient
where PatientName LIKE ('__n%sa')
```

Chapter 6: SQL Operators II

In chapter 5, we were introduced to SQL operators, which help us filter records from the database based on a particular condition. In chapter 5, we studied comparison and logical operators. In this chapter, we are going to study the remaining three types of operators.

Contents

- **Conjunctive Operators**
- **Negation Operators**
- **Arithmetic Operators**

NOTE:

Before executing the queries in this chapter, add five more records in the "Patient" table using the following INSERT statement.

```
INSERT INTO Patient VALUES
```

```
(105, 'Joseph', 26, 'Heart Disease'),
(156, 'Julian', 31, 'Lung Disease'),
(247, 'Margret', 29, 'Heart Disease'),
(259, 'Russ', 47, 'Ear Infection'),
(318, 'Candice', 42, 'Ear Injury')
```

Now your "Patient" table should have following 10 records:

PatientID	PatientName	PatientAge	DiseaseDescription
101	James	10	Heart Disease
105	Joseph	26	Heart Disease
150	Sarah	15	Lung Disease
156	Julian	31	Lung Disease
245	Isaac	21	Kidney Disease
247	Margret	29	Heart Disease
250	Mike	17	Ear Infection
259	Russ	47	Ear Infection
301	Maria	6	Nose Injury
318	Candice	42	Ear Injury

1- Conjunctive Operators

Conjunctive operators are used to connect two or more conditions. Conjunctive operators are primarily used with a "where" clause. There are two conjunctive operators in SQL:

I. AND
II. OR

- **AND**

An AND condition is used to perform a logical AND operation among multiple conditions specified with a "where" clause. With the AND operator, only those records which fulfill all the conditions specified in multiple "where" clauses are retrieved from the database. For example, if you want to retrieve the records of all patients aged greater than 20 and whose DiseaseDescription contains string "Lung", you can use the following query:

Query 1

```
SELECT * FROM Patient
where   PatientAge>20   AND   DiseaseDescription   LIKE
('%lung%')
```

The output of the above query is as follows:

PatientID	PatientName	PatientAge	DiseaseDescription
156	Julian	31	Lung Disease

- **OR**

The OR operator is used to perform a logical OR operation among multiple conditions specified in the "where" clause. For instance, if you want to retrieve the records of all patients aged greater than 20 and having either lung or heart disease, you can extend Query 1 as follows:

Query 2

```
SELECT * FROM Patient
where   PatientAge>20   AND   (DiseaseDescription   LIKE
('%lung%')
OR DiseaseDescription LIKE ('%Heart%') )
```

Here, the use of brackets is particularly important. The last two conditions with the LIKE operator have been encapsulated in round brackets. Therefore, the AND operator will operate between the first condition and the output of the OR will be between the last two conditions. The output of Query 2 is as follows:

PatientID	PatientName	PatientAge	DiseaseDescription
105	Joseph	26	Heart Disease
156	Julian	31	Lung Disease
247	Margret	29	Heart Disease

To see what happens if you remove the brackets around the last two conditions joined by OR, execute the following query:

Query 3

```
SELECT * FROM Patient
where   PatientAge>20   AND   DiseaseDescription   LIKE
('%lung%')
 OR DiseaseDescription LIKE ('%heart%')
```

In Query 3, by default the AND operator will operate between the first and second condition and the OR operator will operate on the result of the "first and second condition" AND the "third" condition. Therefore, in the output you will see the records of all the patients with ages greater than 20 who have lung disease, as well as patients who have heart disease, regardless of age.

PatientID	PatientName	PatientAge	DiseaseDescription
101	James	10	Heart Disease
105	Joseph	26	Heart Disease
156	Julian	31	Lung Disease
247	Margret	29	Heart Disease

2- Negation Operators

The negation operator is used to negate logical operators. They are used to reverse the output obtained through normal logical operators. You simply have to append the NOT before the operator name. Following are some commonly used negation operators:

    I.   != or <> (NOT EQUAL)
    II.   NOT BETWEEN
    III. NOT IN
    IV. NOT LIKE
    V.   IS NOT NULL

To retrieve records of all the patients who do not have heart disease, you can use following NOT LIKE query:

Query 4

```
SELECT * FROM Patient
where DiseaseDescription NOT LIKE ('%heart%')
```

The records of all patients who have diseases other than Heart Disease will be retrieved in the output, which is shown in the table below:

PatientID	PatientName	PatientAge	DiseaseDescription
150	Sarah	15	Lung Disease
156	Julian	31	Lung Disease
245	Isaac	21	Kidney Disease

250	Mike	17	Ear Infection
259	Russ	47	Ear Infection
301	Maria	6	Nose Injury
318	Candice	42	Ear Injury

Similarly, if you want to retrieve the records of all the patients except those with ages less than 30 and greater than 10, you can use the following NOT BETWEEN query:

Query 5

```
SELECT * FROM Patient
where PatientAge NOT BETWEEN 10 and 30
```

It is important to note here is that the records that lie on the boundary are also not included in the retrieved records. For instance, if you have a record with age 30, it will not be retrieved. The output of Query 5 is as follows:

PatientID	PatientName	PatientAge	DiseaseDescription
156	Julian	31	Lung Disease
259	Russ	47	Ear Infection

| 301 | Maria | 6 | Nose Injury |
| 318 | Candice | 42 | Ear Injury |

3- Arithmetic Operator

There are four types of SQL arithmetic operators:

I. Addition (+)
II. Subtraction (-)
III. Multiplication (*)
IV. Division (/)

Arithmetic operators are used to perform mathematical operations on columns that contain numeric data. For instance, you can retrieve the sum of a patient's PatientID and PatientAge using the following query:

Query 6

```
SELECT PatientID + PatientAge as PatientInfo,
PatientID,
PatientAge, PatientName, DiseaseDescription FROM
Patient
```

In Query 6, we obtained the sum of the patients's PatientID and PatientAge and displayed it in the PatientInfo column, followed by all the other columns of the table. The output of Query 6 is as follows:

PatientInfo	PatientID	PatientAge	PatientName	DiseaseDescription
111	101	10	James	Heart Disease
131	105	26	Joseph	Heart Disease
165	150	15	Sarah	Lung Disease
187	156	31	Julian	Lung Disease
266	245	21	Isaac	Kidney Disease
276	247	29	Margret	Heart Disease
267	250	17	Mike	Ear Infection
306	259	47	Russ	Ear Infection
307	301	6	Maria	Nose Injury
360	318	42	Candice	Ear Injury

Exercise 6

Task:

From the "Patient" table, retrieve the records of all patients with ages greater than 30 years who do not have either ear disease or kidney disease. Multiply the age of the retrieved patients by 2 and display it in the ExtendedAge column.

Solution

```
SELECT PatientAge * 2 as ExtendedAge, PatientID,
PatientAge, PatientName, DiseaseDescription FROM
Patient
where PatientAge > 30 AND DiseaseDescription NOT
LIKE ('%ear%')
AND DiseaseDescription NOT LIKE('%kidney%')
```

Chapter 7: Aggregate Functions, Delete, & Update

Up till now, we have been dealing with individual records. We saw how to insert individual records in a database, how to retrieve records from the database based on criteria, and how to apply different types of filters to fetch a desired output. What if we want to retrieve the maximum age of the patients from the PatientAge column? SQL Aggregate functions help us perform this task. We shall see some of the most commonly used aggregate functions in SQL. We shall also see how we can delete records from a table and how we can update existing records.

Contents

- **Aggregate Functions**
    I. Count()
    II. Avg()
    III. Sum()
    IV. Max()

  V. Min()
  VI. First/Top()
  VII. Ucase/Upper()
  VIII. Lcase/Lower()
- **Delete Statement**
- **Update Statement**

1- Aggregate Functions

The following are some of the most commonly used functions.

NOTE:

All the queries in this chapter are executed on the "Patient" table with the 10 records we inserted in the last chapter. (Refer to Chapter 6.)

  I. **Count()**

The Count() function counts the number of rows which satisfy a particular criteria. For instance, if you want to count the number of patients who have Heart disease, you can use Count() function as follows:

Query 1

```
SELECT COUNT(PatientID) as PatientsWithHeartDisease
From Patient
WHERE DiseaseDescription LIKE ('%heart%')
```

The above query counts the patient with heart disease and displays the result in the "PatientsWithHeartDisease" column.

II. Avg()

The Avg() function returns the average of values in a particular table column based on some criteria. For instance, if you want to retrieve the average age of all patients with heart disease, you can employ the Avg() function as follows:

Query 2

```
SELECT AVG(PatientAge) as AverageAgeofHeartDisease
From Patient
WHERE DiseaseDescription LIKE ('%heart%')
```

III. Sum()

The Sum() function returns the sum of the values in a particular table column based on some criteria. For instance, if you want to retrieve the sum of the ages of all patients, you can employ the Sum() function as follows:

Query 3

```
SELECT Sum(PatientAge) as SumOfAges
From Patient
```

IV. Max()

The Max() function returns the maximum of all of the values in a particular table column. For instance, if you want to retrieve the maximum age of all the patients, you can use the Max() function as follows:

Query 4

```
SELECT Max(PatientAge) as MaximumAge
From Patient
```

V. Min()

Similarly, to retrieve the minimum patient age, the following query can be executed:

Query 5

```
SELECT Min(PatientAge) as MaximumAge
From Patient
```

VI. Top/First()

The Top() or First() functions return the top 'n' of all of the values in a particular table column, where "n" is any integer. For instance, if you want to retrieve the age of the first three patients in the "Patient" table, you can use the Top() function as follows:

Query 6

```
SELECT Top 3 PatientAge as First3Ages
From Patient
```

The above query will retrieve the ages of the first three patients. The output will look like this:

First3Ages
10
26
15

To retrieve the ages of the last three patients in the "Patient" table, you can use the Top() query in conjunction with the "Order By" clause as follows:

Query 7

```
SELECT Top 3 PatientAge as Last3Ages
From Patient Order by PatientAge desc
```

The output of Query 7 is as follows:

Last3Ages
47
42

VII. Upper()/Ucase

The Upper() or Ucase() function converts all the values in the selected column to uppercase. This function applies only to columns with string or character values.

Query 8

```
SELECT Upper(PatientName) as PatientNameUpper
From Patient
```

The output of Query 8 is as follows:

PatientNameUpper
JAMES
JOSEPH
SARAH
JULIAN
ISAAC
MARGRET

MIKE
RUSS
MARIA
CANDICE

VIII.   Lcase()/Lower()

Similarly, to convert column values to lower case, the Lcase() or Lower() function is used. Since I am using MS SQL Server for demonstration purposes, I will use Lower() in my Query.

Query 9

```
SELECT Lower(PatientName) as PatientNameLower
From Patient
```

The output will contain all the PatientName values in lower case as follows:

PatientNameLower
james
joseph

sarah
julian
isaac
margret
mike
russ
maria
candice

2- Delete Statement

We know how to insert records into a database; we also know how to retrieve records using a SELECT statement and how to filter records using a "where" clause with various SQL operators. Now we will learn how to delete records from the table.

To delete records, the SQL DELETE statement is used. Like the SELECT statement, the DELETE statement can also be used in conjunction with a SELECT statement to delete filtered records. Let's look at how we can delete all the records from the table. To do so, the following query can be executed:

Query 10

```
DELETE From Patient
```

This query will delete all the records from the patient table. However, in some scenarios, we want only records that satisfy particular criteria to be deleted. For instance, you can delete the records of all patients with heart disease using the following query:

Note: Before executing this query, you should have 10 records in the "Patient" table, which we inserted in the last chapter.

Query 11

```
Delete From Patient
where DiseaseDescription like('%heart%')
```

The above query will delete all the patient records which have heart disease in the DiseaseDescription column.

3- Update Statement

We know how to insert, retrieve, and delete records; in this section, we shall learn how to update an existing record. To update a record, the UPDATE statement is used in SQL, followed by the SET keyword, which is used to update an existing value.

If you want to replace the string "Heart Disease" in the DiseaseDescription column with the string "Cardiac Disease", you can use an UPDATE statement as follows:

Query 12

```
UPDATE Patient
SET DiseaseDescription = 'Cardiac Disease'
where DiseaseDescription like('%heart%')
```

Exercise 7

Task:

Delete the records of all patients aged greater than 30 who have ear diseases. Set the age of all patients with lung disease to 40.

Solution

Deleting Records

```
Delete From Patient
where PatientAge > 30 AND DiseaseDescription LIKE ('%ear%')
```

Updating Records

```
UPDATE Patient
set PatientAge = 40
where DiseaseDescription LIKE ('%lung%')
```

Chapter 8: Relationships & Join Queries

Up to this point, we have been executing all our queries on a single table. However, real life databases contain hundreds, or even thousands, of tables. These tables are associated with each other via relationships. In Chapter 1 of this book, I gave you a glimpse at how database tables are linked with each other. We saw how the "Student" table was associated with the "Department" table via a column, DID, which stored the ID of the department to which student belonged. This is one type of database relationship. In this chapter, we shall study different types of database relationships and Join queries.

Contents

- Table Relationships
    I. One-to-One Relationship
    II. One-to-Many Relationship
    III. Many-to-Many Relationship

- Join Statements
    I. Inner Join
    II. Left Join
    III. Right Join
    IV. Outer Join
- Group By
- Having

1- Table Relationships

Database tables can be linked with each other via one of the three types of relationships.

- **One-to-One Relationship**

In a "one-to-one" relationship between two tables, for every record in the first table, there is exactly one record in the second table. The Primary key of the first table exists as the Foreign key in the second table and vice versa. For example, there is a "one-to-one" relationship between the "Employee" table and the "Pension" table, since one Pension record belongs to one Employee and one Employee can have only one Pension record. In most scenarios, "one-to-one" relationships are removed by merging the data into a single column.

Note:

A Foreign key is basically a column in the table which stores the primary key of the table with which it is linked. In Chapter 1, we saw that the Student table had a column labeled DID, which stored the ID of the department to which a student belonged.

- **One-to-Many Relationship**

In a "one-to-many" relationship, against one record in the first table, there can be multiple records in the second table. In a "one-to-many" relationship, the table on the "many" side of the relationship is stored as a Foreign key and the Primary key of the table is on the "one" side of the relationship. The relationship between the "Department" and "Student" tables is the perfect example of a "one-to-many" relationship, since one department can have multiple students. In the "Student" table, many records can have one department.

- **Many-to-Many Relationships**

In "many-to-many" relationships, for one record in the first table, there can be multiple records in the second table; for one record in the second table, there can be multiple records in the first table. The relationship between the "Author" and "Book" tables is a good example of "many-to-many" relationships. A book can be written by multiple authors while an author can write multiple books. In most cases, "many-to-many" relationships are broken down into "one-to-many" relationships by creating an intermediate table that has "one-to-many" relationships with both the actual tables.

2- Join Statements

Join statements are used to select column values from two or more tables which are linked with each other. For instance, take a scenario where you have to display the names of students along with the names of the departments to which they belong. However, there is no department name column in the "Student" table; it only contains the department ID, which serves as a Foreign key to Department. Therefore, we need some mechanism to select column values from multiple tables which are linked together. JOIN queries help us perform this function.

Before executing JOIN queries, run the following script in your query window.

Script 1

```
Create Database School

Use School
Go


CREATE TABLE Student
  (StudID int PRIMARY KEY NOT NULL,
   StudName varchar(50) NOT NULL,
   StudentAge int NULL,
   StudentGender varchar(10) NOT NULL,
       DepID int NULL)

CREATE TABLE Department
  (DepID int PRIMARY KEY NOT NULL,
   DepName varchar(50) NOT NULL,
       DepCapacity int NULL)

ALTER TABLE Student ADD CONSTRAINT StudDepRel FOREIGN KEY ( DepID) references Department(DepID)

INSERT INTO Department Values
(1, 'English', 100),
(2, 'Math', 80),
(3, 'History', 70),
(4, 'French', 90),
(5, 'Geography', 100),
(6, 'Drawing', 150),
```

(7, 'Architecture', 120)

INSERT INTO Student Values
(1, 'Alice', 21, 'Male', 2),
(2, 'Alfred', 20, 'Male', 3),
(3, 'Henry', 19, 'Male', 3),
(4, 'Jacobs', 22, 'Male', 5),
(5, 'Bob', 20, 'Male', 4),
(6, 'Shane', 22, 'Male', 4),
(7, 'Linda', 24, 'Female', 4),
(8, 'Stacy', 20, 'Female', 1),
(9, 'Wolfred', 21, 'Male', 2),
(10, 'Sandy', 25, 'Female', 1),
(11, 'Colin', 18, 'Male', 1),
(12, 'Maria', 19, 'Female', 3),
(13, 'Ziva', 20, 'Female', 5),
(14, 'Mark', 23, 'Male', 5),
(15, 'Fred', 25, 'Male', 2),
(16, 'Vic', 25, 'Male',null),
(17, 'Nick', 25, 'Male',null)

The above script will create a new database, School, with two tables, "Department" and "Student". A "one-to-many" relationship has been defined between the "Department" and "Student" tables using following query:

ALTER TABLE Student ADD CONSTRAINT StudDepRel FOREIGN KEY (DepID) references Department(DepID)

The above query states that, in the Student column, a Foreign key constraint named "StudDepRel" (you can use any name) will be added, which sets the DepID column of the Student table as a Foreign key which references the DepID column of the Department table.

After you run Script 1, you should have "Department" and "Student" tables containing following data:

Department Table

DepID	DepName	DepCapacity
1	English	100
2	Math	80
3	History	70
4	French	90
5	Geography	100
6	Drawing	150
7	Architecture	120

Student Table

StudID	StudName	StudentAge	StudentGender	DepID

1	Alice	21	Male	2
2	Alfred	20	Male	3
3	Henry	19	Male	3
4	Jacobs	22	Male	5
5	Bob	20	Male	4
6	Shane	22	Male	4
7	Linda	24	Female	4
8	Stacy	20	Female	1
9	Wolfred	21	Male	2
10	Sandy	25	Female	1
11	Colin	18	Male	1
12	Maria	19	Female	3
13	Ziva	20	Female	5
14	Mark	23	Male	5
15	Fred	25	Male	2
16	Vic	25	Male	NULL

| 17 | Nick | 25 | Male | NULL |

- INNER JOIN

INNER JOIN (also called JOIN) retrieves data from the selected column from both tables if, and only if, there exists a common value in both tables in the column specified by the JOIN condition. For instance, to retrieve the names of students from the student column along with their department names from the department column, the following INNER JOIN query is used:

Query 1

```
SELECT Student.StudName, Department.DepName
From Student
Join Department
On Student.DepID = Department.DepID
```

The output of the above query is as follows:

StudName	DepName
Alice	Math
Alfred	History
Henry	History
Jacobs	Geography

Bob	French
Shane	French
Linda	French
Stacy	English
Wolfred	Math
Sandy	English
Colin	English
Maria	History
Ziva	Geography
Mark	Geography
Fred	Math

You can see only those records from the "Student" and "Department" tables have been retrieved where there was a common value in the DepID of the "Student" table and the DepID of the "Department" table. The last two records from the "Student" table have not been retrieved, since there is no corresponding DepID. Similarly, the last two records from the

"Department" table have also not been retrieved, since they are not referenced by any of the records in the "Student" table.

- **LEFT JOIN**

LEFT JOIN retrieves all the records from the first table and only those records from the second table where a common value exists in both tables, as specified by the JOIN condition. For instance, the following query retrieves all the records from the "Student" table and only those records from the "Department" table where there is a corresponding DepID value in the "Student" table.

Query 2

```
SELECT Student.StudName, Department.DepName
From Student
Left Join Department
On Student.DepID = Department.DepID
```

The output of Query 2 is as follows:

StudName	DepName
Alice	Math
Alfred	History
Henry	History
Jacobs	Geography

Bob	French
Shane	French
Linda	French
Stacy	English
Wolfred	Math
Sandy	English
Colin	English
Maria	History
Ziva	Geography
Mark	Geography
Fred	Math
Vic	NULL
Nick	NULL

You can see that the last two students don't have any corresponding DepID, yet they have been retrieved.

- **RIGHT JOIN**

RIGHT JOIN retrieves all the records from the second table and only those records from the first table where a common value exists in both tables, as specified by the JOIN condition. For instance, the following query retrieves all the records from the "Department" table and only those records from the "Student" table where there is a corresponding DepID value in the "Department" table.

Query 3

SELECT Student.StudName, Department.DepName
From Student
Right Join Department
On Student.DepID = Department.DepID

StudName	DepName
Stacy	English
Sandy	English
Colin	English
Alice	Math
Wolfred	Math
Fred	Math
Alfred	History

Henry	History
Maria	History
Bob	French
Shane	French
Linda	French
Jacobs	Geography
Ziva	Geography
Mark	Geography
NULL	Drawing
NULL	Architecture

- **FULL JOIN**

FULL JOIN is the union of RIGHT JOIN and LEFT JOIN. FULL JOIN retrieves all records from both tables, whether or not a match is found between the Foreign key and Primary key of the linked table. Have a look at the following query:

Query 4

```
SELECT Student.StudName, Department.DepName
```

```
From Student
Full Join Department
On Student.DepID = Department.DepID
```

The output of the code in Query 4 is as follows:

StudName	DepName
Alice	Math
Alfred	History
Henry	History
Jacobs	Geography
Bob	French
Shane	French
Linda	French
Stacy	English
Wolfred	Math
Sandy	English
Colin	English

Maria	History
Ziva	Geography
Mark	Geography
Fred	Math
Vic	NULL
Nick	NULL
NULL	Drawing
NULL	Architecture

3- Group By

The "Group By" statement allows us to group data based on results from some aggregate functions. For instance, if you want to display the name of each department along with the average age of the student from that department, you can use a "Group By" statement as follows:

Query 5

```
SELECT    Department.DepName,    AVG(Student.StudentAge)    as AverageStudentAge
From Student
Right Join Department
On Student.DepID = Department.DepID
```

Group by DepName

The above query will calculate the average age of students belonging to each department and will display them against each department's name.

DepName	AverageStudentAge
Architecture	NULL
Drawing	NULL
English	21
French	22
Geography	21
History	19
Math	22

4- Having

Since a "Where" clause cannot be used to filter data grouped by aggregate functions, the "Having" statement was introduced in the SQL. For instance, if you want to retrieve the names of only those departments where the average age of students is greater than 20, you can use a "Having" statement as follows:

Query 6

```
SELECT      Department.DepName,      AVG(Student.StudentAge)      as AverageStudentAge
From Student
Right Join Department
On Student.DepID = Department.DepID
Group by DepName
Having AVG(Student.StudentAge) > 20
```

The result of Query 6 is as follows:

DepName	AverageStudentAge
English	21
French	22
Geography	21
Math	22

Exercise 8

Task:

For each department, display the department name and maximum age of students in that department if the age is between 21 and 24.

Solution

```
SELECT Department.DepName, Max(Student.StudentAge) as Age
 From Student
Right Join Department
On Student.DepID = Department.DepID
Group by DepName
Having Max(Student.StudentAge) Between 21 AND 24
```

Chapter 9: SQL Sub-queries

Until now, we have been executing single SQL queries to perform insert, select, update, and delete functions. However, there is a way to execute SQL queries within the other SQL queries. For instance, you can select the records of all the students from the database with an age greater than a particular student. In this chapter, we shall demonstrate how we can execute sub-queries or queries-within-queries in SQL.

Let's jump straight into our first example. Remember, for this chapter we are using the "School" database which we created in Chapter 8. You should have tables labled "Student" and "Department" with some records.

Suppose we want to retrieve the names of all students whose age is greater than "Stacy"; we can do so by two methods. First, we can retrieve the Stacy's age, store it in some variable, and then, using a "where" clause, compare the age in our SELECT query. The second approach is to embed the query which retrieves

Stacy's age inside the query which retrieves the ages of all students. The second approach employs a sub-query technique. Have a look at Query 1 to see sub-queries in action.

Query 1

```
Select * From Student
where StudentAge >
(Select StudentAge from Student
where StudName = 'Stacy'
)
```

Notice in Query 1 we have used round brackets to append a sub-query in the "where" clause. The above query will retrieve the records of all students from the "Student" table where the age of the student is greater than age of "Stacy". The age of "Stacy" is 20; therefore, in the output, you shall see the records of all students aged greater than 20. The output is as follows:

StudID	StudName	StudentAge	StudentGender	DepID
1	Alice	21	Male	2
4	Jacobs	22	Male	5
6	Shane	22	Male	4
7	Linda	24	Female	4
9	Wolfred	21	Male	2

10	Sandy	25	Female	1
14	Mark	23	Male	5
15	Fred	25	Male	2
16	Vic	25	Male	NULL
17	Nick	25	Male	NULL

Similarly, if you want to update the name of all the students with department name "English", you can do so using sub-query as follows:

Query 2

```
Update Student
Set StudName = StudName + ' Eng'
where Student.StudID in (
        Select StudID
        from Student
        Join
        Department
        On Student.DepID = Department.DepID
        where DepName = 'English'
)
```

In the above query, the student IDs of all the students in the English department have been retrieved using a JOIN statement in the sub-query. Then, using an UPDATE statement, the names of all those students have been updated by appending a string "Eng" at the end of their names. A WHERE statement has been used for matching the student IDs retrieved by using a sub-query.

Now, if you display the Student name along with their Department name, you will see "Eng" appended with the name of the students belonging to English department.

Exercise 9

Task:

Delete the records of all students from the "Student" table where student's IDs are less than the ID of "Linda".

Solution

```
Delete From Student
where StudID <
(Select StudID from Student
where StudName = 'Linda'
)
```

Chapter 10: SQL Character Functions

SQL character functions are used to modify the appearance of the retrieved data. Character functions do not modify the actual data; rather, they only perform certain modifications in the way data is represented. SQL character functions operate on string type data. In this chapter, we shall some of the most commonly used SQL character functions.

Note:

All of the queries in this chapter are executed on the School database created in Chapter 8.

- **Concatenation (+)**

Concatenation functions are used to concatenate two or more strings. To concatenate two strings in SQL, the '+' operator is used. For example, we can join student names and student genders from the student column and display them as one column as follows:

```
Select StudName +' '+StudentGender as NameAndGender
from Student
```

- **Replace**

The replace function is used to replace characters in the output string. For instance, the following query replaces "ac" with "rs" in all student names.

```
Select StudName, REPLACE(StudName, 'ac', 'rs') as ModifiedColumn
From Student
```

The first parameter in the replace function is the column whose value you want to replace; the second parameter is the character sequence which you want to replace, followed by third parameter which denotes the character sequence you want to be inserted in place of the old sequence.

- **Substring**

The substring function returns the number of characters starting from the specified position. The following query displays the first three characters of student names.

```
Select StudName, substring(StudName, 1, 3) as SubstringColumn
From Student
```

The first parameter in the substring method is the column name, the second parameter is the starting index from where you want to get the substring, and the third parameter is the number of characters you want to fetch.

- **Length**

The length function is used to get the length of values of a particular column. For instance, to get length of names of students in the "Student" table, the following query can be executed:

```
Select StudName, Len(StudName) as NameLength
from Student
```

Note that, in the above query, we used the Len() function to get the length of the names; this is because in the SQL server, the Len() function is used for calculating the length of any string.

- IFNULL

The IFNULL function checks if there is a Null value in a particular Table column. If a NULL value exists, it is replaced by the value passed as the second parameter to the IFNULL function. For instance, the following query will display 50 as the department ID of the students with a null department ID.

```
Select Student.DepID, IFNULL(Student.DepID, 50)
from Student
```

- LTRIM

The LTRIM function trims all the empty spaces from the values in the column specified as parameters to the LTRIM function. For instance, if you want to remove all the empty spaces before the names of the students in the "Student" table, you can use the LTRIM query as follows:

```
Select Student.StudName, LTRIM(Student.StudName)
from Student
```

- RTRIM

The RTRIM function trims all the proceeding empty spaces from the values in the column specified as parameters to the RTRIM function. For instance, if you want to remove all the empty spaces that come after the names of the students in the "Student" table, you can use the RTRIM query as follows:

```
Select Student.StudName, RTRIM(Student.StudName)
from Student
```

Exercise 10

Task:

Replace 'a' with 'z' in all the students's names that end with 'd'. Display the actual student names and replaced student names on screen.

Solution

```
Select StudName, REPLACE(StudName, 'a','z')
from Student
where StudName LIKE ('%d')
```

Other Books by the Author

JavaScript Programming: A Beginners Guide to the Javascript Programming Language
http://www.linuxtrainingacademy.com/js-programming

If you've attempted to learn how to program in the past, but hadn't had much success then give *JavaScript Programming* a try. It will teach you exactly what you need to know about programming in the world's most widely used scripting language in existence today. It will start you at the beginning and allow you to build upon what you've learned along the way.